Head Above The Economy

7 Proven Techniques to Mastering Survival in a Shifting Economy

Eric Graham

Copyright © 2024 Eric Graham

All Rights Reserved. No part of this publication may be scanned, uploaded, reproduced, stored in a retrieval system or transmitted in any form or by any means: electronic, mechanical, photocopy, recording, or otherwise without the express written permission of the author or publisher except in the case of brief quotations in a book review.

DEDICATION

I dedicate this book to my lovely wife in taking care of the house for me to work on this material.

ACKNOWLEDGEMENT

I am grateful to God Almighty for His leading by His Holy Spirit in helping me put this material together.

I am also grateful for all the individuals who have helped in making this project a reality:

Contents

DEDICATION 3

Introduction 1

When Ends Don't Meet 7

Making Every Dollar Count 21

Side Hustles and Smart Moves 33

The Debt Dilemma 43

The Power of Less 55

Investing in Uncertain Times 63

Thriving Together in Tough Times 73

Conclusion 89

Introduction

Our entire lives are impacted by the economy, in all its complexity. We all experience the effects in one way or another, whether it's the rising price of groceries, the volatility of petrol costs, or the difficulty of saving for the future.

Nevertheless, some people appear to handle these with grace and confidence in spite of the uncertainties. What is their trade secret? When others feel overburdened, overextended, or in survival mode, how do they manage to stay ahead of the economy?

For anyone looking for direction, strategy, and optimism during uncertain financial times, this book is more than just one of the many guides that exist—it's a lifeline. It stands out. Head Above the Economy is about empowerment, not just numbers and budgets.

It involves figuring out how to adjust to changes in the economy without losing sight of your objectives. It's about learning how to survive while preserving your dreams, peace, and self-respect.

In actuality, there will always be changes in the economy. There will always be opportunities and challenges. How you react is what makes your experience unique. Even in the most difficult financial situations, you may use the techniques in this book to go from just surviving to flourishing. Every chapter serves as a lighthouse, showing the route to stability, financial resilience, and eventually growth.

Consider yourself in an aisle of a grocery store, deciding whether to return the box of cereal that has increased in price by $2 from the previous week. Or think of a family who must make the painful choice to leave their cherished house due to the rent going through the roof. These are common difficulties, not unique experiences. Although the effects of economic hardship vary from person to person, they are universal.

Nowadays, many families have to deal with the fact that they can get more out of a dollar than they could in the past. Expenses appear to be growing faster than wages.

Even the most well-laid financial plans can be derailed by an unforeseen bill or a sudden loss of employment. The repercussions affect not just our financial situation but also our relationships, sense of security, and mental health.

Anyone who has ever pondered how to make ends meet when the math simply doesn't add up should read this book. It is intended for people who are struggling with debt, budgeting, or generating new sources of money. It is intended for people who aspire to financial independence but are unsure of where to begin.

Why This Book Is Important

Your financial difficulties are not unique to you, and you don't have to deal with them on your own. The ideas presented in Head Above the Economy are derived from timeless wisdom, real-life experiences, and helpful guidance. Every chapter addresses a particular issue and deconstructs it into manageable actions that anybody may take.

We'll look at the why as well as the how. Why do some people recover from financial difficulties while others don't? Why does financial resilience result from particular behaviors and attitudes? This book offers solutions by fusing relevant tales, professional views, and firsthand experiences.

Each chapter is meant to motivate and prepare you. The techniques presented here will change the way you interact with money and the economy, from budgeting to investigating side projects, from streamlining your life to making prudent investments.

This is what you should expect in the subsequent pages of this book;

When Ends Don't Meet: Understanding the True Impact of Economic Strain

Explore the emotional and practical effects of financial hardship and learn how families adapt creatively to overcome challenges.

The Budget Balancing Act: Making Every Dollar Count

Learn how to align your spending with your priorities, set clear goals, and take control of your finances through effective budgeting.

Side Hustles and Smart Moves: Creating Multiple Streams of Income

Discover how to turn skills into income, balance side hustles with life, and build financial resilience through diversification.

The Debt Dilemma: Breaking Free Without Breaking Down

Gain strategies to tackle debt systematically and learn how to transform your financial mindset for lasting freedom.

The Power of Less: Simplifying Life to Stay Ahead

Simplify your financial and personal life to reduce stress, focus on essentials, and achieve greater peace and stability.

Investing in Uncertain Times: Small Steps Toward Big Gains

Approach investing with confidence by starting small, making informed decisions, and staying steady in a volatile market.

The Community Connection: Thriving Together in Tough Times

Harness the power of collective support, shared resources, and collaboration to create opportunities and build resilience.

As you dive into this book, I encourage you to reflect on your current financial situation and the steps you can take to improve it. Ask yourself: What changes can I make today to ensure a better tomorrow? The journey ahead is not about perfection but progress.

With determination, knowledge, and a clear plan, you can rise above the challenges of the economy. You can keep your head above the shifting tides and move confidently toward a brighter financial future.

Chapter 1

When Ends Don't Meet

"The way we spend our money defines the way we live."
– Ruth Soukup

The market had shifted so drastically in such a short period of time that I was astounded. My wife and I made the decision to launch a small bakery and beverage business back in 2022. We were enthusiastic and optimistic, not only concerned about how we could transform our passion for drinks and baking into something worthwhile, we needed to establish side businesses to support our paycheck.

One significant obstacle, though, was that we were unable to find a store in a desirable area. We looked everywhere, but every potential location was either too costly or previously occupied. Despite our disappointment, we made the decision to take a break and try again later when the time seemed appropriate.

As at 2024, and at the time of writing this book, we considered that decision again. In the hope that the market might have changed or at least stayed the same, my wife and I made the decision to try the business again. But we were dumbfounded by what we found. Not only was the world of 2024 different, but it was completely different.

I can very clearly recall entering the store to get prices on some of the products we required. We paid about $12 for the same package of butter in 2022, but it now costs more than $50. I initially believed it to be an error or perhaps an attempt by one store to overcharge. However, everywhere we went, it was the fact. We were left in shock as we saw item after thing and price after price.

I had the impression that I was dreaming and that when I woke up, everything would be as it had been. However, it was real and not a dream. In just two years, the economy had changed so dramatically that we began to wonder how anyone could afford to continue operating a business, much less launch a new one.

It was difficult to comprehend the shock of it all, but I knew I had to come to terms with it. Making a complaint wouldn't make things simpler or alter the costs. Whether my wife and I are prepared or not, the world is constantly changing, and we must constantly figure out how to overcome the obstacles it presents. We started the business any ways, but everything was different, I tell you.

The Rising Cost of Living: When Paychecks Aren't Enough

You might be aware of this fact that over the previous few years, the expense of living has progressively climbed. And for many of us, it doesn't only feel like paychecks aren't enough to cover the necessities anymore, it is the order of the day. Isn't that what is happening.

And we are not just talking about luxury products or frills that you don't need—the topic is about the necessities. Rent, groceries, petrol, and utilities have all become more expensive. It feels that no matter how much you work or how hard you try to save, your income just doesn't go as far as it used to.

It's a frustrating scenario. You can find yourself making tough choices every month. Do you buy that extra thing your family needs, or do you save it for the next pay period? Do you cut back on eating out, or do you sacrifice something else, like entertainment or social activities, to keep the lights on?

These are the hard decisions many of us are facing. The expense of living isn't just about prices going up—it's also about the feeling of being trapped in a cycle where no matter how hard you strive; things never feel quite enough.

Wages have not been increasing at the same rate as inflation, which is a large part of the problem. You may be getting paid the same amount, but the price of basic products is growing.

For instance, your monthly shopping expenditure might have been $300 last year, but this year, it's closer to $400 for the same list of things. Rent might feel like a hefty burden, especially when home prices continue to grow, while incomes are stagnant.

Now, what can we do about it? The first step is to admit the reality. Many people don't realize how much the growing cost of living impacts them until they see their salary and the bills side by side. It's necessary to take a step back and thoroughly analyze where your money is going.

Understanding your spending will help you take control. Cutting back isn't easy, but it's vital when you're living on a budget. It could be hard to forgo certain indulgences, but in the long run, it's better than overextending yourself financially.

One way to help cope with the rising cost of living is to boost your income. This could entail taking on a side hustle or exploring ways to make more at your existing employment.

In today's society, there are so many opportunities to earn additional cash, whether it's freelancing, teaching, or driving for a ridesharing service. The goal isn't necessary to make a fortune but to make up the difference between what you're making and what you need to live comfortably.

Another approach is to take a closer look at your budget and see where you can minimize costs. Maybe you don't need that subscription service anymore, or you can make coffee at home instead of buying it every day. Small changes might pile up over time. But the trick here is to keep adaptable. The economy is continuously evolving, so your financial plan needs to be adaptable.

You may not have perfect control over your money, but you can manage how you spend.

By recognizing the issue, making modifications to your budget, and finding new ways to improve your income, you may better handle the rising cost of living. It won't be easy, but you can survive—and even thrive—despite these financial obstacles

From Comfort to Crisis: How Economic Shifts Hit Home

At one time, everything was at ease. Your work was secure, your bills were moderate, and life appeared steady. But then, an economic shift happens—a recession, a layoff, inflation—and suddenly, comfort feels like a distant memory. What was once easy becomes difficult. A few changes in the economy, and everything you took for granted starts to feel precarious.

These economic shifts don't simply effect big firms; they affect families, too. It's tempting to think of a crisis as something far away, something that occurs to others, but it can happen to everyone. A sudden job loss, the cost of living rising unexpectedly, or even a shift in interest rates might put your financial stability off course. The sensation of having a secure future is swiftly replaced with anxiety about how to make ends meet.

The issue in times of economic upheaval is that they often occur unannounced. One day, your firm might announce layoffs, or gas prices could increase, and suddenly, you find yourself facing a financial catastrophe. If you're already living paycheck to paycheck, any substantial move in the economy can feel like a calamity. It can feel as though your whole world is coming apart because all your plans were predicated on the idea that things will stay steady.

But it's crucial to recognize that this is not the end of the trip. Yes, an abrupt shift can throw you off balance, but it doesn't have to break you. In these moments, the most important thing to do is keep cool and assess your options. You might have to tighten your budget, discover ways to minimize spending, or even seek for additional ways to bring in money. But worrying won't help you survive the crisis—it's about making wise, informed judgments.

One of the first things you should do when facing an economic shift is to review your emergency reserves. If you've been saving for a rainy day, now is the time to use it. If you haven't saved up, this is the wake-up call to start doing so as soon as possible. A decent rule of thumb is to have enough funds to cover three to six months of living expenses.

Another technique is to become more flexible. In times of economic instability, adaptability is your strongest tool. If your industry is struggling, it may be time to consider other career options or pick up a part-time work. Learning new skills or gaining additional training might help you remain competitive in the employment market. It's about doing whatever it takes to stay afloat as the economy rebounds.

Lastly, don't disregard your mental health. Financial stress may take a big toll on your mental well-being. Take time to relax, interact with loved ones, and seek the help you need. When things feel unclear, the most essential thing is to stay strong and cheerful, knowing that with a little tenacity, you can overcome whatever comes your way.

Silent Sacrifices: What Families Give Up to Stay Afloat

When money is tight, families typically make concessions. Sometimes, these sacrifices are obvious—like cutting out trips or eating out less. But frequently, the most meaningful sacrifices are modest, unrecognized by others but deeply felt.

It could be giving up a pastime, skipping a night out with friends, or not buying the new clothes the kids require. These sacrifices may not seem like much on the surface, but over time, they mount up and start to damage your family's happiness.

In many households, the financial hardship can mean that something needs to give. Parents can skip buying new clothes or forgo medical appointments only to make sure the bills get paid. These are the silent sacrifices that happen behind the scenes. The sacrifices can take an emotional toll, too. Constantly worrying about money can lead to stress, anxiety, and even friction between family members. Everyone feels it, but nobody talks about it.

These compromises don't simply effect adults—they harm children too. When money is limited, youngsters may not understand why they can't have the same items as their friends. This can lead to emotions of inadequacy or animosity.

As a parent, it's crucial to explain the dilemma without overwhelming your children, but also to make them feel part of the solution. It's not just about cutting down; it's about teaching children the value of money, how to budget, and how to save.

Despite the sacrifices, families can still find ways to be cheerful. It's vital to remember that material things aren't the only method to show love and caring. Spending quality time together, even if it's just a walk in the park or a homemade meal, can help develop family relationships. Sometimes, the greatest present you can give your family is the gift of presence and unity.

While making compromises to keep afloat is painful, it may also be an opportunity for growth. As a family, you may learn to value what really matters—your health, your relationships, and your ability to support one another.

Even though financial sacrifices may appear harsh, they can eventually bring a family closer together. And once things improve, you'll all have a stronger appreciation for the things that actually count.

- **Reflection Questions:**

How have changes in your income or expenses affected your daily life and well-being?

What sacrifices have you made to keep up with the rising costs of living?

How can you take control of your financial situation instead of letting it control you?

Chapter 2

Making Every Dollar Count

"A budget is telling your money where to go instead of wondering where it went." – *John C. Maxwell*

Because of the sharp increase in costs for products on the market, my wife and I soon came to the conclusion that every dollar we spent needed to be carefully considered if we wanted the business to survive. There was absolutely no room for mistake or child's play.

The whole business could fall apart in a few weeks, or even days, if we were reckless with our spending. We have no space to mess up, I tell you. Though we needed money to support our paycheck, the business was about creating something important with each other, not just about making money.

I started to be critical about how we handled things. My wife assumed responsible for maintaining thorough records of all expenditures. Prior to making any purchases, we had to budget for each item we required. We looked for the most cost-effective strategies to operate the company without sacrificing quality for our clients. We adhered to it even though it wasn't easy.

Although the first few weeks weren't easy, things started to get better gradually. Consumers were pleased, and word got out. We saw things begin to shift in our favor by implementing these concepts and paying close attention to every little detail. Although the difficulties persisted, we managed to overcome them.

Needs vs. Wants: Redefining Priorities in Tough Times

In tight financial times, you must decide between needs and wants. We're used to having stuff at our fingertips, so it's easy to mix the two. However, when money is scarce, needs and wants matter more.

Needs are essential. Survival or daily functioning depends on it. Consider food, water, shelter, healthcare, and transportation. These sustain your life. Wants, on the other hand, make life more comfortable or joyful, but you can live without them. Wants include new phones, nice dinners, and the latest fashions.

When money is limited, the problem is learning to prioritize your needs. The first step is to take a thorough look at your budget. Go over your costs and categorize them into needs and wants. It may be uncomfortable at first, especially when you discover exactly how many items you've been spending on that you don't genuinely need. But this approach is vital to gain control of your finances.

For example, let's imagine you're used to eating out several times a week. While this may feel like a necessity since it's easy, it's actually a want, not a need. Cooking meals at home can save you a significant amount of money.

Another area where many individuals overspend is entertainment. While it's crucial to relax and enjoy life, items like streaming subscriptions, movie tickets, or dining out might be scaled back in tight times.

Once you've determined your needs and wants, it's time to make some tough choices. Cutting back on wants doesn't mean you can't enjoy life—it means finding more economical methods to appreciate what you love. You may trade expensive dinners for picnics in the park, or find free events in your region instead of going to overpriced concerts or movies.

Redefining your priorities can not only help you manage your finances better but also provide you peace of mind. When you focus on the necessities, you'll feel more in control, less anxious, and more secure in your ability to weather rough financial circumstances. By learning to say no to the things that are lovely but not necessary, you're investing in your future and your financial well-being.

Stretching Thin: Creative Ways to Cut Costs

When you're already stretched thin financially, the concept of decreasing costs could seem insurmountable. But there are always ways to make things work if you're imaginative and prepared to look outside the box. Cutting costs doesn't mean fully losing your quality of life—it just means being smarter with how you spend.

The first place to start is by examining your normal spending. Some of them are fixed, like rent or your car payment, but others are more variable, like groceries, utilities, or entertainment. Look for areas where you can pare down without feeling deprived. For example, if you're paying for a premium cable package, consider moving to a more reasonable streaming provider. Or if you're buying groceries without a plan, start meal planning to avoid wasting food.

One excellent technique to save money is by negotiating. Many individuals don't understand that firms are often prepared to cut your bill if you simply ask. Whether it's your internet, phone plan, or even your rent, pick up the phone and inquire if there are any discounts or promotions available. The worst they can say is no, but you might be amazed at how often you can save just by asking.

Another inventive cost-saving suggestion is to embrace DIY (do it yourself) solutions. Instead of paying for pricey services, try tackling certain activities on your own. For example, instead of hiring someone to clean your home, set aside a few hours each week to clean yourself. If you're handy with tools, consider basic home repairs yourself instead of paying a professional.

You can also save by buying old things instead of new ones. Whether it's clothes, furniture, or electronics, second-hand things can be just as excellent as new, sometimes at a fraction of the price. Thrift stores, online marketplaces, and garage sales are fantastic venues to locate bargains.

One last tip is to cut down on spontaneous buying. Impulse purchase is one of the fastest ways to squander your budget. To avoid this, establish a list before you go shopping and stick to it. If you're online buying, take a moment to pause and think about whether you truly need the item. A simple 24-hour rule—waiting a day before buying something non-essential—can help you avoid wasteful purchases.

By being resourceful and searching for ways to decrease costs, you may stretch your budget without compromising the things that matter most. It's all about being intentional with your money, planning ahead, and making modest changes that build up over time. With a little innovation, you may find methods to save without feeling like you're living in deprivation.

Every Penny Matters

When it comes to managing money, it's easy to fall into the trap of thinking tiny expenses don't matter. A coffee here, a snack there—it all adds up, right? But many people disregard the potential of little saves, assuming they won't make a major difference in the long term. The truth is, every penny does matter, and recognizing this mindset adjustment is vital to regaining control over your finances.

It's not just about being tight with money—it's about building a healthy relationship with your spending. Every time you choose to save rather than spend, you're making an investment in your future. Small savings can increase over time, and even a little bit of discipline can lead to major changes in your financial status.

The first thing to do is to track your spending. Many people don't recognize where their money is going until they see it on paper. You might be astonished to find out how much you're spending on items like snacks, coffee, or subscription services that you don't even use. Start by jotting down every expense, no matter how minor. Once you see the amount, you'll understand how quickly tiny expenses may pile up.

Next, start prioritizing your spending. Instead of aimlessly spending on minor items, ask yourself if it's something you genuinely need or if it's just a want. Every time you say no to a needless purchase, you're making a conscious decision to save. It's not about depriving yourself; it's about making smarter decisions.

To encourage this thinking shift, consider about your financial goals. Do you want to save for a vacation, pay off debt, or develop an emergency fund? Visualizing these goals will help you stay motivated to save, especially when it feels like minor sacrifices won't make a difference. Each penny saved puts you one step closer to realizing your dreams.

Another strategy to modify your perspective is by focusing on long-term financial wellness. It's easy to rationalize little spending now, but when you look at the wider picture, you'll see how those small actions might affect your future. By being attentive of every dime you spend, you're building a foundation for financial stability and freedom.

Ultimately, the mindset adjustment is about taking control of your finances. It's not about living paycheck to paycheck or constantly worrying about money. It's about being intentional with your spending, saving when you can, and recognizing that every little bit counts. By changing the way you think about money, you can make a meaningful difference in your financial future.

- **Reflection Questions:**

What areas of your spending are currently not aligned with your financial priorities?

Have you created a budget that reflects your values and long-term goals?

What small adjustments can you make today to improve your financial situation?

Chapter 3
Side Hustles and Smart Moves

"Don't put all your eggs in one basket." – *Proverb*

Turning Skills Into Cash: What's in Your Hands?

When money is tight, it's tempting to feel that there's nothing you can do to improve your financial condition. But here's the truth: you have abilities, and those skills can be turned into revenue. Everyone has something they're good at, whether it's writing, cooking, organizing, or simply chatting to people. The key is understanding that what you already know how to accomplish can become a source of revenue.

The first step is to take inventory of your skills. What do you enjoy doing? What are you naturally good at? Maybe you're exceptional at graphic design, or perhaps you adore instructing younger pupils in arithmetic. Maybe you're the go-to person in your family for fixing stuff around the house. Whatever it is, there's undoubtedly someone out there who would be willing to pay you for that expertise.

For example, let's imagine you're incredibly good at social media and marketing. Instead of just using your social media accounts for enjoyment, you may offer your skills to local businesses or individuals who need help with their online presence. If you're great at writing, consider freelance writing. There are websites where firms publish writing jobs that you may apply for. If you're handy with tools, you may start a small repair business. The options are infinite.

You don't need a degree or years of expertise to get started. Many people have transformed simple skills into full-fledged businesses just by starting small. Maybe you don't have a great website or a vast portfolio, but you have the skill, and that's the most crucial aspect. The benefit of turning your skills into revenue is that you get to work on your own terms. You can start small and build up over time, steadily increasing your income as you go.

One of the most important things to remember is to ask for what you're worth. It can be frightening to place a price tag on your expertise, but remember that what you offer has value. Don't sell yourself short. It's alright to start with a small price, but make sure you're charging enough to make it worth your effort.

Ultimately, turning skills into cash is about being resourceful and inventive. What's in your hands right now could be the route to financial freedom. You don't need a big budget or sophisticated equipment—just your skills and the courage to put them to work.

Small Starts, Big Impact

We all know that great success stories may be encouraging, but it's easy to forget that most people didn't start big. They started small, with a lot of hustle and even more guts. It's not about having the perfect circumstances or waiting for everything to be just right; it's about taking action with what you've got and moving forward, no matter how small the steps may appear.

Think about the tale of persons like Oprah Winfrey or Steve Jobs. They didn't become successful overnight. Oprah started as a news anchor, and Steve Jobs started in a garage. The secret to their success was persistent effort, even when the odds were stacked against them. They worked hard with what they had and kept going when things became rough. It wasn't easy, and it didn't happen quickly—but they continued moving forward.

The same can be true for you. Maybe you're establishing a side employment or a tiny business, and it feels like you're not getting anywhere. But remember, every small step adds up. Maybe you're only receiving a few clients here and there, or you're still working out the best method to market yourself. That's okay. Every day you invest in effort is a day closer to accomplishing your objective.

Look upon the minor victories. Did you get a positive review from a customer? Celebrate it! Did you figure out how to improve your process? That's a win! Those tiny triumphs develop confidence and momentum, which are crucial to long-term success.

Success doesn't necessarily come from making great jumps. Sometimes it's the modest steps, the steady hustle, and the daily struggle that lead you to where you want to be. The most essential thing is not to give up. Don't compare your trip to others—just keep your concentration on your own road and keep working toward your goals.

And remember: your hustle doesn't need to look like anyone else's. The influence you create, no matter how minor it seems now, might be significant in the long term. Just keep going forward and stay consistent. Over time, those tiny steps will lead to enormous rewards.

The Time Trade-Off

When you're juggling a full-time job plus side gigs, it can feel like there's just not enough time in the day. The reality is, balancing side gigs and your personal life is tricky. But it's not impossible. It only involves a little bit of organization, a lot of time management, and realizing that something has to give sometimes.

The first thing you need to know is that time is a scarce resource. You only have so many hours in a day, and it's tempting to overcommit, especially when you're trying to expand your side business. But if you're not careful, you might quickly find yourself burnt out and overwhelmed. That's why it's vital to set clear boundaries for your side gigs and your personal time.

Start by scheduling your time. Set aside particular hours for your side hustle and keep those hours sacred.

When you're working on your side gig, be fully present. When it's time to be with family or friends, make sure you're mentally checked in. By putting limits around your time, you can lessen the stress of feeling pulled in several ways.

It's also crucial to analyze how much time you're spending on your side employment against your personal life. If your side gig is taking up too much time and harming your relationships, it may be time to reassess. Are there things you can delegate or automate? Can you work more efficiently to free more time for the things that matter? Sometimes it's not about working harder—it's about working smarter.

Another method to balance is by being realistic about what you can handle. It's tempting to take on any opportunity that comes your way, especially when you're excited about your side hustle. But learning to say no when you're stretched thin is a crucial ability. You can't do everything, and that's okay. By focusing on the most important duties and being judicious about what you take on, you'll be able to maintain a healthy balance.

Finally, remember that self-care is vital. You won't be able to perform your best in your side gig if you're burned out. Take time to rest, exercise, and enjoy your life outside of work. By taking care of yourself, you're guaranteeing that you'll have the energy and focus to offer your side business the attention it needs.

Balancing side gigs and life is a juggling act, but with the appropriate methods, it's possible to thrive in all domains. Set boundaries, manage your time properly, and don't forget to take care of yourself. With time and experience, you'll find the balance that works best for you.

Reflection Questions:

What skills or talents could you turn into a profitable side hustle?

How can you balance a side hustle with your full-time responsibilities without burning out?

What steps can you take to diversify your income streams and reduce financial vulnerability?

Chapter 4

The Debt Dilemma

"Debt is the slavery of the free." – *Publilius Syrus*

I guess you may be wondering why we didn't try the business again in 2023 after we couldn't make it work in 2022. Why did we have to wait until 2024? The answer is simple but painful: debt. We really wanted to give it another shot in 2023, but something held us back, and you can guess what it was. Debt had us almost drowning.

How we got into such a situation is a long story, and to narrate everything would take more space than this book can allow. But here's the summary: we had tried another business before, one we believed in with all our hearts. Regretfully, things didn't work out. In addition to losing every penny we had invested, we also lost the money of others.

The failure of that business left us in a financial mess that took over a year to clean up. It wasn't just the loss of money; it was the emotional weight of knowing we had to face each new day with the burden of debt hanging over us. There were opportunities we could see, opportunities we could even smell, but we couldn't grab them because we were tied down. Debt became the wall between us and every chance to start fresh.

We spent 2023 doing everything we could to get out of that hole. It wasn't easy. There were sleepless nights, moments of frustration, and days when we felt like giving up. But we kept going, step by step, paying back what we owed, and finding ways to regain control of our finances. Slowly, we began to see progress.

By 2024, we finally felt ready to try again. It wasn't just about having the money to invest—it was about having the courage to believe in ourselves after such a big failure. Starting the pastries and beverages business wasn't just a decision; it was a statement that we wouldn't let debt define us.

The Weight of Debt: Why It Feels Like a Trap

With every day that goes by, debt might feel like an invisible burden that gets heavier. The stress, anxiety, and ongoing pressure are just as much a part of it as the money you owe. Have you ever felt like no matter how hard you work or how much you try to save, the debt keeps hanging over you? That's because debt doesn't just take away your money—it also takes away your peace of mind.

When you have debt, it feels like a trap since there's no fast escape. The monthly payments roll in, and it seems like you're perpetually behind. You make an effort to reduce your expenses, yet the bills continue to mount. It feels like you're jogging in place.

Your paychecks don't stretch far enough to cover everything, plus you're constantly juggling between the essentials: rent, groceries, utilities, and the ever-present debt payments. No matter how much you work, it's hard to see a route out.

Debt can also establish a cycle. The more you owe, the harder it is to save. The harder it is to save, the more you rely on credit. It's a vicious spiral, and each turn makes the trap feel tighter. The invoices stack up, the interest increases, and soon, you're not just paying for what you borrowed—you're paying for the fees and interest on top of it all.

But it's not just about the money—it's about the worry that comes with it. Debt might impair your mental health. The constant concern can keep you up at night, worried about how to make ends meet or how to get ahead. It can lead to anxiety and even depression. Debt takes away your confidence. You may start feeling like you're not in control, that you'll never get ahead, and that you'll constantly be locked in this loop.

And let's not forget the emotional toll it takes on your relationships. Money troubles can put strain on marriages, families, and friendships. Arguments regarding finances can lead to resentment, remorse, and frustration. It's not only about the money; it's about the trust and security you feel in your personal life. Debt affects everything, not just your wallet.

So, why does it feel like a trap? Because it can be overwhelming. The weight of debt is more than just the balance you owe. It's the constant push to keep afloat. But just because it feels like a trap doesn't imply it's permanent. Understanding the impact debt has on your life is the first step toward breaking free. You can take charge.

Finding Your Way Out

When it comes to paying off debt, it's easy to feel overwhelmed. There are so many ways to approach it, and it can be hard to figure out where to start. Two prominent ways are the snowball method and the avalanche method, and both have their strengths. So, how can you determine which one is right for you?

The snowball strategy is all about modest gains. You start by paying off your smallest loan first, regardless of the interest rate. The idea is to develop momentum. Once you pay off one loan, you feel accomplished. That feeling of victory inspires you to tackle the next obligation, and the cycle continues. It's like rolling a snowball downward. The more you pay off, the bigger the ball gets, and before you realize it, you've made tremendous progress.

One of the key benefits of the snowball method is psychological. When you're facing a pile of debt, it's easy to feel discouraged. But by starting with the least debt, you get to taste the joy of achievement early on. It can provide the drive you need to keep going, especially if you're someone who needs that instant win to stay motivated.

On the other hand, the avalanche strategy is all about saving money on interest. With the avalanche strategy, you focus on paying off the debt with the greatest interest rate first, regardless of the size. The idea is to limit the amount of money you spend on interest, which helps you pay off your obligations faster in the long run. While the avalanche technique may take longer to show results, it can save you a lot of money over time.

The benefit of the avalanche method is financial. By tackling high-interest bills first, you're minimizing the entire cost of your debt. You may not see the minor wins right away, but you're making major progress in the most effective way imaginable.

So, which one should you choose? It depends on what you value more: psychological gains or financial efficiency. If you need motivation to keep going, the snowball method can be your best bet. But if you want to save the most money and get rid of your debt as rapidly as possible, the avalanche method might be the preferable alternative.

Remember, the most essential thing is to stick to your plan. No matter the strategy you select, consistency is crucial. Set your objective, stay devoted, and you'll get there.

Living Free

Imagine waking up in the morning without the weight of debt hanging over you. No more stressing about how to pay the bills, or where the next income is coming from. That sensation of independence is possible, and it's one of the best joys of becoming debt-free.

Debt independence isn't simply about the financial relief. It's about the emotional calm that comes with it. When you're debt-free, you have more control over your life. You may make choices without the continual concern of falling behind. You can sleep better at night knowing that you're not weighted down by financial worry.

Living free from debt also means having the flexibility to focus on what matters most. Without debt, you can focus your energy into things that offer you joy—whether it's spending time with family, pursuing a passion, or working toward new goals. You're no longer living in survival mode. You can take risks, make plans, and build a future that's not controlled by the need to pay off loans or credit cards.

And let's not forget the impact on your relationships. Financial stress is one of the primary causes of friction in marriages and families. When debt is no longer a burden, you can focus on building trust, spending quality time together, and creating memories. You're not constantly arguing over money. Debt freedom helps you to cultivate your relationships and generate a sense of security and happiness in your life.

But the emotional pleasures go beyond just feeling well. Debt liberation offers a sense of success. It's the consequence of hard effort, planning, and sacrifice. When you attain that objective, you learn that you're capable of far more than you believed. It's a reminder that you have the capacity to change your circumstances and take control of your destiny.

So, while the road to debt freedom may be lengthy and tough, the rewards are worth it. Financial peace, mental comfort, greater relationships, and a brighter future are all within your reach. It's not just about being debt-free; it's about living free—and that's priceless.

Reflection Questions:

How has debt impacted your mental and emotional well-being?

What small steps can you take today to begin tackling your debt, even if it feels overwhelming?

How can you reframe your relationship with money to avoid accumulating more debt in the future?

Chapter 5
The Power of Less

"The ability to simplify means to eliminate the unnecessary so that the necessary may speak." – *Hans Hofmann*

Declutter Your Finances: Letting Go of What Doesn't Serve You

Has the sheer quantity of things in your life ever made you feel overwhelmed? Do you mean the heaps of useless items, the old clothing that takes up room, or the messy workstation that is constantly piled high with paperwork? Well, your finances can become just as messy, and it may make managing your money feel just as burdensome. It's time to conduct some financial decluttering.

When it comes to finances, decluttering means taking a long hard look at everything you're spending money on. Think of it as cleaning out your closet. There are things in there you haven't worn in years but yet cling on to, just in case. S

Similarly, you can have subscriptions you don't utilize or insurance coverage you don't need. These things might be minor, but when you add them all up, they start to swallow a major piece of your money.

Start by examining your monthly expenses. Take a moment to note everything you're paying for, even if it's just a few bucks here and there. You'll be shocked by what you find. Maybe it's an unused gym subscription or that streaming service you rarely watch. These tiny things pile up, and before you realize it, they're eating into your budget.

Once you've discovered these "clutter" charges, ask yourself: Does this actually serve me? If the answer is no, let it go. It's okay to cancel subscriptions or stop buying goods that aren't providing value to your life. Just like decluttering your home offers more room and clarity, cleaning up your finances allows you to focus on what actually important.

The idea here is to streamline your spending so that you may focus your money on items that bring you joy or help you attain your financial goals. Sometimes, cleaning your money involves getting rid of the unneeded stuff, so you can make way for things that will take you forward. You'll be shocked at how much lighter and more focused you feel once you start letting go of what doesn't serve you.

The Joy of Less

In a world that continually tells us we need more—more possessions, more money, more things to keep up with—it might be hard to think that less could truly be more. But what if I told you that simplifying your financial life may bring you more freedom than you ever dreamed possible?

Think about that for a moment. Have you ever bought anything you didn't really need, just because it was on sale or because everyone else had it? Maybe it was a trendy gadget, a new pair of shoes, or a membership service you didn't really utilize. Sure, it felt wonderful for a while, but did it genuinely add value to your life? Did it make you happier or more fulfilled? Often, the answer is no.

When we focus less on accumulating new things and more on enjoying what we already have, we begin to achieve freedom. The delight of fewer doesn't just extend to physical stuff. It also pertains to how we handle money. It's about being intentional with what we spend and making sure every purchase corresponds with our values and aspirations.

Simplifying your finances involves cutting back on the impulsive buys, the unneeded spending, and the things that don't really offer value to your life. It can involve lowering your lifestyle or learning to live with less. But that doesn't imply forsaking comfort or happiness. On the contrary, it implies you're releasing yourself from the incessant strain of requiring more to feel satisfied.

Living with less provides you the opportunity to focus on what actually matters—whether it's establishing an emergency fund, saving for the future, or investing in activities that bring joy. It means you're no longer weighed down by the weight of unnecessary financial burdens. You're free to focus on the things that genuinely make your life richer, not just your money account.

Making Space for What Truly Matters

How often do we make space in our life for what actually matters? In the rush and bustle of daily life, it's easy to get distracted by what looks essential rather than what's vital. The same is true with your finances.

If you're continuously pursuing the next big buy or getting caught up in spending just to keep up, you might be missing the greater picture.

Making space for what actually matters comes with figuring out what that is. For some folks, it's building a secure financial future. For others, it's creating experiences with loved ones or giving back to organizations they care about. But no matter what your priorities are, making space for them entails aligning your spending with your principles.

Start by asking yourself what's most essential to you. Is it your family? A comfortable retirement? Paying off debt? Once you know your priorities, you can begin to change your budget and spending patterns to reflect those principles. You might realize that some of the things you've been spending money on are distractions, driving you away from your true goals.

One of the finest ways to create room for what matters is by removing financial clutter. This can involve cutting back on impulse purchases, canceling needless subscriptions, or even downgrading services you don't truly need. By reducing the superfluous, you free up more resources—time, energy, and money—for the things that are most meaningful to you.

Making room also requires learning to say no to things that don't correspond with your aims. It can be hard to resist the push to buy or keep up with trends, but by saying no to the unneeded, you're saying yes to the things that matter most. Whether it's saving for a large goal, investing in a passion, or spending time with family, the freedom to focus on what matters will pay off in the long term.

By cleaning your finances and making space for your priorities, you generate the room to develop a life that represents what you genuinely care about. It's about living with intention and letting go of the distractions that drag you away from your best life.

Reflection Questions:

What unnecessary expenses or possessions could you let go of to simplify your life?

How can simplifying your financial life help you focus on what truly matters?

In what areas of your life can you apply the principle of "less is more" to achieve greater peace?

Chapter 6

Investing in Uncertain Times

"The stock market is filled with individuals who know the price of everything, but the value of nothing." – *Philip Fisher*

Starting Small: Why Every Investment Counts

The adage "It's not about how much you start with, it's about how you start" may be familiar to you. This is especially true when it comes to investing. Because they believe it takes a lot of money to get started, many people steer clear of investing. In actuality, though, it's okay to start small—in fact, it's the greatest way to get your feet wet.

Let's dissect it. Investing can be compared to planting a tree. You don't have to immediately plant a massive, fully developed tree. Rather, you sow a tiny seed and tend to it. With time and attention, it develops into something much larger. That seed is your first little investment. It might not seem like much at first, but it might develop into something significant over time.

Even with a modest investment, it makes a difference. Begin with your financial means. Every little step forward puts you on the correct track, regardless of the amount—ten, fifty, or one hundred dollars. The important thing is to start since that first action establishes a saving and investment habit. Your investments will have more time to grow if you start early.

It's also crucial to keep in mind that making little investments allows you to gain experience. You risk making costly mistakes if you jump into large investments too soon. You can become accustomed to the process and progressively learn how to make better selections by starting small. Before hopping into a fast sports car, it's similar to learning to drive a modest, manageable car.

You can also benefit from compound interest with little investments. At this point, your investment income begins to increase on its own. Your modest investments will eventually begin to generate income for you, and that income will then generate even more income. Over time, this snowball effect can have a profound impact.

In the end, starting small does not guarantee that you will remain tiny. Every major investor started out with a little sum of money and worked their way up. Consistency is crucial. You may lay a solid foundation for financial success by beginning small and being steady.

High-Reward, Low-Risk Strategies for Regular Investors

It's not necessary for investing to feel like gambling. To see strong returns, you don't need to take big risks. In actuality, low-risk investments can be among the best ones. Let's discuss safe strategies that can nevertheless yield profitable outcomes.

Index funds are among the simplest low-risk investment options available. You are not investing all of your money in a single company because these investments combine a large number of various stocks. This reduces the risk because the other stocks in the fund may still do well even if one does not. Because they are easy to invest in and have a track record of providing consistent returns over time, index funds are widely used.

Bonds are another low-risk choice. In essence, you are giving money to the government or a business when you purchase bonds, and they agree to repay you with interest. Although the gains might not be as great, bonds are thought to be safer than stocks since they provide more consistent returns. But with less risk, they're a fantastic way to keep your money increasing.

A smart strategy for novice investors is to concentrate on so-called "blue-chip stocks." These are stock holdings in sizable, reputable businesses with a solid performance history. Consider corporations such as Coca-Cola, Microsoft, or Apple. These businesses are more established than smaller, riskier ones, and even while their stock values might not rise dramatically overnight, they have been in business for a long time.

Another low-risk investment choice is real estate. You might invest in real estate investment trusts (REITs), but I'm not saying you have to purchase a mansion or commercial property. With them, you can invest in real estate without really owning it. Without having to cope with the inconveniences of upkeep or tenant management, you can still receive a portion of the proceeds from the sale or rental of your home.

Finding the balance is essential to low-risk, high-reward investing. In addition to making sure your investments are secure, you also want them to increase in value over time. You can reduce your risk while still earning some respectable profits by selecting safer, more diversified investments.

Riding the Waves: Maintaining Consistency Amid Economic Volatility

The economy and stock market can occasionally feel like roller coasters. There are times when everything seems to be falling apart, and other times when everything are soaring. When things are going well, it's tempting to get swept up in the excitement, and when they start to go south, it's simple to panic. However, the secret to investing well is to understand how to maintain your composure at both highs and lows.

First and foremost, it's critical to recognize that markets inherently fluctuate. This is quite typical. Consider it like the weather: occasionally it rains, and other times it's sunny. Investments are no different. When things appear to be going badly, the best course of action is to remain calm. The last thing you want is to lock in losses by selling your investments during a downturn.

Instead, concentrate on your long-term objectives. Investors that are successful are aware that the market always recovers in the end. You'll probably see your investments increase over time if you stick with them. One of the most crucial qualities for an investor is patience. You risk missing out on long-term gains if you're always attempting to time the market by buying and selling in response to transient fluctuations.

Diversifying your portfolio also helps. This entails distributing your money throughout several asset classes, such as equities, bonds, and real estate. Your overall wealth is protected because other parts of the market may be doing well when one is struggling. Similar to eating a well-balanced meal, diversification involves consuming a variety of meals to make sure you're getting all you need, even if one nutrient isn't there.

It is tempting to panic and withdraw your investments during difficult economic circumstances. But keep in mind that maintaining stability requires having a well-defined plan and following it. Remind yourself that ups and downs are a natural part of the trip and stay focused on your financial objectives. Maintaining stability will probably result in financial success in the long run.

Ultimately, having patience and a plan are the keys to riding the market's waves. Avoid letting fear influence your choices. You're more likely to succeed in the long run if you can maintain your composure under pressure.

Reflection Questions:

What are your current thoughts on investing, and how can you approach it with more confidence?

How can you make informed, yet conservative, investment decisions during uncertain times?

What steps can you take to start investing, even with a small budget?

Chapter 7

Thriving Together in Tough Times

"Alone we can do so little; together we can do so much."
– Helen Keller

It wasn't easy sailing in the boat of debt. It isn't easy at all. Looking back, I often wonder how we managed to stay afloat during those turbulent times. For me, I thank God every day for the good support I had from my wife. She wasn't just a partner in our successes; she stood by me through the failures too.

She was in the same boat, of course, because we got into the debt together. But beyond that, her understanding and unwavering support made all the difference. She never blamed me or gave up on us, even when the pressure was overwhelming. Every step we took to climb out of that hole, she was there—encouraging, strategizing, and reminding me that we would come out stronger.

Apart from her, my elder brother became a pillar of support for us during that difficult season. To be honest, without him, I'm not sure what we would have done. Our debtors were on us, demanding payment. The shame of it all could have overwhelmed us, and we had nothing to offer them. When we most needed him, my brother came through for us, protecting us from the shame that was about to descend upon us.

He didn't just help us from a distance; he carried our burden as though it was his own. He had sleepless nights because of us. I could see it in his eyes and hear it in his voice. He felt the weight of our debt as if it were his own. In truth, he wore our clothes—he stepped into our shoes and bore the full brunt of the situation without holding back.

I can't describe how much that meant to me. Knowing that someone else cared enough to share our pain gave us the strength to keep moving forward. My brother's sacrifice wasn't just about money; it was about the love and selflessness he showed when we needed it most.

Through it all, I thank God for the support we had during that moment. Without my wife's understanding and my brother's help, I don't know how we would have made it. Those were dark days, but their support gave us light and hope to keep pressing on.

The Power of Networks: Strength in Shared Resources

We are all aware that life can surprise us with unexpected turns, and leveraging the strength of networks is one of the finest strategies to deal with these difficulties.

Having a solid support system around you might be crucial when you're going through a difficult time, be it a financial crisis, personal difficulties, or even a job setback. A network's assistance can be a lifeline during difficult times, offering both emotional and practical support.

Let's discuss what networking actually entails. It goes beyond simply having a list of contacts or a large social circle. Building sincere, trustworthy connections where individuals support one another is the essence of true networking.

You might know someone who can offer you advise on your career, or they might have a friend who is knowledgeable about financial tactics. This mutual understanding and readiness to assist are priceless.

Asking for favors when you need them isn't the only way to develop a strong network. It also involves lending a hand to those in need. Mutual assistance is the foundation of a strong network.

The bonds that hold you to other people are strengthened when you are able to give back. Better opportunities may arise later on when you most need them. Giving and receiving are more important than merely taking from your network.

Consider yourself going through a difficult period, possibly one that involves money. Your network can help by offering guidance on managing your debt, creating a budget, or even providing resources that could make ends meet.

It's possible that a friend of yours who works in a different industry can supply information on fresh employment openings or freelancing work. Additionally, networks can provide emotional support. Knowing that you have individuals you can talk to who are sympathetic to your plight is reassuring.

Networking doesn't have to be difficult, which is the best part. It all comes down to interacting with like-minded individuals and being genuine. The caliber of the relationships you form is more important than knowing hundreds of individuals. Mutual regard, trust, and a willingness to support one another are the cornerstones of a robust network.

It's critical to keep in mind that networking requires sustained engagement. It takes time to develop relationships. You must work hard, be interested in other people, and lend a hand when you can. You'll discover that your network gets stronger and your available resources increase in value over time.

Networks are even more important during difficult times. Whether you're having financial difficulties, mental health problems, or job obstacles, your network can offer helpful support. They can provide you guidance, point you in the direction of fresh prospects, and provide emotional support when times seem hopeless. You can't undervalue the strength that comes from having others on your side.

In certain situations, your network may even be able to provide material resources, tools, or even cash assistance. Perhaps you lack the necessary tools and require assistance with a side project.

A buddy could know where you can get inexpensive tools to rent, or they might have an additional set of tools they could offer you. When you're feeling stuck, these tiny but important acts of resource sharing might help you get past your obstacles.

Mutual assistance, shared resources, and trust are the foundation of a robust network. It's about developing relationships that will support you when you need them and lending a helping hand to others when they need it.

You'll have more support when times are hard if you put more effort into your network. Whether you need financial assistance, emotional support, or even practical counsel, having a strong network can help you face life's obstacles head-on.

Why Teamwork Is Better in Times of Crisis Than Competition

Many of us have an innate desire to compete when things get hard. Competition frequently seems like the best option, whether it's for a job, a promotion, or even a money opportunity. However, this might not be the ideal way of thinking in a crisis. In actuality, cooperation is frequently a far more effective strategy than rivalry. Here's why.

People are fighting for their lives during a crisis, whether it is a worldwide pandemic, a personal hardship, or an economic depression. Nobody succeeds by attempting to outdo one another at a moment like this. Rather, teamwork enables everyone to use their resources, expertise, and abilities to solve problems. We can all benefit from additional opportunities if we work together.

Consider companies during the COVID-19 pandemic, for instance. Many businesses were in survival mode at first. Previously exclusive competitors began pooling their resources. They worked together to figure out how to keep their customers satisfied, their businesses open, and their employees productive. They may share inventions and cut expenses by collaborating with rivals, which would be advantageous to both sides.

Collaboration can be just as advantageous on a personal level. Working with people who are experiencing similar financial difficulties can help you come up with new solutions. For example, a group of friends may gather together to discuss ways to save expenses, identify new revenue streams, or even combine resources to work toward a common objective, like launching a side business.

However, cooperation involves more than just resource sharing; it also involves mutual learning. Working together exposes you to fresh viewpoints, abilities, and ideas that you may not have previously thought of. For instance, someone in your network may have helpful advice on how to prioritize bills, bargain with creditors, or create a debt payback plan if you're attempting to manage your debt but don't know where to begin.

Collaboration also creates a sense of community during difficult times. It serves as a reminder that you are not alone. Everybody experiences something, and when we work together, we demonstrate that we are all in this together. Working as a team provides emotional support that can boost motivation and lessen stress. It may be simpler to persevere if you know that you have a support system that is sympathetic to your difficulties.

In the end, cooperation makes resilience possible. The collective gains strength when everyone cooperates. The others can step in and provide assistance even if one person is having difficulties. This provides a safeguard against the challenges that accompany a crisis. By working together, you benefit not only yourself but also other members of your community. Additionally, it is simpler to overcome adversity when everyone rises together because of their combined strength.

Therefore, keep in mind that competition might not be the solution the next time you find yourself in a difficult situation. Instead, concentrate on working with others. Distribute your expertise, assets, and abilities. You'll discover that managing the difficulties you encounter becomes considerably simpler when you collaborate, and everyone engaged gains from the team effort.

Creating an Effective Support Network

We all have difficulties in life, and it's easy to feel isolated when things get difficult. However, creating a network of support is one of the finest strategies to overcome obstacles in life. A strong support network keeps you anchored when everything else seems unclear, provides direction when you're unsure, and catches you when you fall. It's similar to having a safety net.

Determining who should be a part of a support system is the first step in creating one. It takes more than just having a large social circle to have a solid support system. It all comes down to surrounding yourself with individuals who truly care about your welfare. Family members, close friends, mentors, or coworkers are examples of people who not only sympathize with your difficulties but also wish to support you in overcoming them.

A strong support network is reciprocal. You must be there for others when they need you, even though you depend on them for support. The foundation of solid, long-lasting relationships is mutual support. This improves the ties within your support system by fostering a reciprocal sense of value and appreciation for all.

A strong support network relies heavily on trust. You may talk openly about your difficulties, voice your worries, and seek assistance without worrying about being judged when you have faith in those around you. Although it takes time to build trust, once it happens, it serves as the cornerstone of your support network. It's hard to rely on those around you when you need them most if you don't trust them.

In a support system, communication is also essential. Never hesitate to ask for assistance when you need it, even if it's only someone to chat to. Most of the time, people want to help, but they might not know how unless you tell them what you need. Your support network will get stronger the more you communicate with it, whether that support takes the form of guidance, money, or simply listening.

However, providing assistance during emergencies isn't the only function of your support network. It's also about encouraging one another to develop. A solid support network should motivate you to reach your objectives, develop your abilities, and be your best self. These individuals will help you achieve greater things, whether it's by giving you career guidance, encouraging you to maintain your financial objectives, or just being there for you when things go hard.

It takes time, effort, and trust to establish a support network. It all comes down to surrounding yourself with caring individuals who are ready to lend a hand, whether it be emotionally or practically. By fostering these connections, you build a support system that will make overcoming obstacles in life easier.

Never forget that you don't have to face life's challenges by yourself. You can develop a strong support network one step at a time, and it can help you get through even the most trying situations.

Reflection Questions:

How has community support helped you during difficult times?

What steps can you take to build a stronger support network in your life?

How can you collaborate with others to create more opportunities for success?

Conclusion

As we reach the end of *Head Above the Economy: Mastering Survival in a Shifting Economy*, it's time to reflect on the journey we've undertaken together. The world of finances, especially in today's unpredictable landscape, can feel overwhelming. Rising costs, fluctuating markets, and economic uncertainties challenge us daily, threatening our stability and peace of mind. Yet, as this book has shown, hope exists in the knowledge, strategies, and resilience we bring to the table.

Imagine standing amidst a storm, buffeted by wind and rain, but knowing you have the tools to weather it. This book equips you with those tools—not to avoid the storm but to face it with confidence. Every decision you make, whether in budgeting, earning, saving, or investing, is a step toward maintaining control over your financial future.

Survival in a challenging economy is not about wealth alone; it's about mindset, discipline, and community.

It's about understanding the balance between what you have and what you can create. It's about simplifying, strategizing, and sometimes sacrificing. Above all, it's about mastering the art of keeping your head above the economy, no matter how turbulent the waters.

Summarizing the Journey: Key Lessons from Each Chapter

- **When Ends Don't Meet: Understanding the True Impact of Economic Strain**

    Life's curveballs, like job losses or sudden expenses, can shake even the most stable households. This chapter taught us to recognize the deep impact of financial strain and find creative, proactive ways to adapt, from cutting back luxuries to seeking community support.

- **The Budget Balancing Act: Making Every Dollar Count**

    Budgeting isn't just about cutting costs; it's about aligning your spending with your values and goals. This chapter encouraged us to reassess priorities, set clear financial plans, and take small yet impactful steps toward financial stability.

- **Side Hustles and Smart Moves: Creating Multiple Streams of Income**

  Relying solely on one source of income can be risky. We explored how side hustles—whether selling handmade goods or leveraging professional skills—can diversify earnings, empower us financially, and provide security in uncertain times.

- **The Debt Dilemma: Breaking Free Without Breaking Down**

  Debt may feel like an endless trap, but it isn't insurmountable. By adopting proven methods like the snowball approach and shifting our money mindset, we learned how to chip away at debt and reclaim our financial freedom.

- **The Power of Less: Simplifying Life to Stay Ahead**

Simplification isn't about deprivation but about focus. By letting go of unnecessary expenses and clutter, this chapter revealed how simplifying can bring emotional relief, financial clarity, and a better quality of life.

- **Investing in Uncertain Times: Small Steps Toward Big Gains**

    Investing doesn't require immense wealth; it requires knowledge, patience, and small, consistent steps. This chapter guided us on starting with modest investments and maintaining composure through economic ups and downs.

- **The Community Connection: Thriving Together in Tough Times**

    No one has to face economic challenges alone. This chapter highlighted the strength in collaboration, sharing resources, and building a robust support network to create collective resilience and opportunities.

Think back to the beginning of this book. Perhaps you felt trapped, overwhelmed, or uncertain about your financial future. Now, you stand equipped with practical strategies, inspiring stories, and a fresh perspective on managing money and navigating economic challenges. Each chapter offered actionable insights to help you adapt and thrive.

As you close this book, don't let it be the end of your journey. Let it be the beginning of a new chapter where you apply what you've learned to secure your financial future. Reflect on the lessons, take actionable steps, and embrace the power within you to rise above challenges.

Remember, the economy may shift and change, but with the right mindset and tools, you can always keep your head above it.

www.ingramcontent.com/pod-product-compliance
Lightning Source LLC
Chambersburg PA
CBHW050324230526
45471CB00005B/2344